W9-CKI-580

Little KITCHEN of HORRORS

CAT LITTER CAKE and Other HORRIFYING DESSERTS

Ali Vega

Lerner Publications ◆ Minneapolis

Lerner Publications Company
A division of Lerner Publishing Group, Inc.
241 First Avenue North
Minneapolis, MN 55401 USA

For reading levels and more information, look up this title at www.lernerbooks.com.

Main body text set in Tw Cen MT Std.
Typeface provided by Monotype.

Library of Congress Cataloging-in-Publication Data

Names: Vega, Ali, author.
Title: Cat litter cake and other horrifying desserts / by Ali Vega.
Description: Minneapolis : Lerner Publications, [2017] | Series: Little kitchen of horrors | Audience: Ages 7-11. | Audience: Grades 4 to 6. | Includes bibliographical references and index.
Identifiers: LCCN 2016019123 (print) | LCCN 2016020251 (ebook) | ISBN 9781512425741 (lb : alk. paper) | ISBN 9781512428056 (eb pdf)
Subjects: LCSH: Desserts--Juvenile literature. | Cooking--Juvenile literature. | LCGFT: Cookbooks.
Classification: LCC TX773 .V44 2017 (print) | LCC TX773 (ebook) | DDC 641.86--dc23

LC record available at https://lccn.loc.gov/2016019123

Manufactured in the United States of America
1-41342-23286-8/31/2016

Photo Acknowledgments
The images in this book are used with the permission of: © Aldo Murillo/iStockphoto, p. 4; © Mighty Media, Inc., pp. 5 (top left), 5 (top right), 5 (bottom), 9 (left), 9 (right), 10, 11 (top), 11 (middle), 11 (bottom), 12, 13 (top), 13 (middle), 13 (bottom), 14, 15 (top), 15 (middle), 15 (bottom), 16, 17 (top), 17 (middle), 17 (bottom), 18, 19 (top), 19 (middle), 19 (bottom), 20, 21 (top), 21 (middle), 21 (bottom), 22, 23 (top), 23 (middle), 23 (bottom), 24, 25 (top), 25 (middle), 25 (bottom), 27 (top), 27 (middle), 27 (bottom), 28, 29 (top), 29 (middle), 29 (bottom); © Elena Elisseeva/Shutterstock Images, p. 6; © Catherine Yeulet/iStockphoto, p. 7; © Digital Vision/Thinkstock, p. 8; © Hill Street Studios/Thinkstock, p. 30.

Front Cover: © Mighty Media, Inc.

CONTENTS

DiSGUSTING DESSERTS

Imagine digging a fork into a freshly baked cake covered in creamy frosting. Picture biting into an apple with an ooey-gooey candy coating, or snacking on a big bowl of jiggly gelatin. Sounds sweet, right? Now imagine that cake is smothered in blood instead of frosting. Or the apple is coated in tar, and the gelatin looks like slimy snot. Would you still eat these treats? Yes, if you knew how great they would taste!

Many people delight in being frightened by food. From a cake that looks like it is topped with cat droppings to cereal treats that look like raw meat, revolting recipes are tons of fun to make and eat. So roll up your sleeves and prepare to make sickening desserts that are supersweet!

Before You
GeT STaRTeD

Cook Safely! Creating disgusting desserts means using many different kitchen tools and appliances. These items can be very hot or sharp. Make sure to get an adult's help whenever making a recipe that requires use of an oven, stove, or knife.

Be a Smart Chef! Cooking gross desserts can be messy. Ask an adult for permission before starting a new cooking project. Then make sure you have a clean workspace. Wash your hands often while cooking. If you have long hair, be sure to tie it back. Make sure your guests don't have any food allergies before cooking. Adjust the recipes if you need to. Make sure your disgusting desserts are safe to eat!

Tools You'll Need

Cooking can involve special tools and appliances. You will need the following items for these disgusting recipes:

- blender
- microwave
- mixer or hand mixer
- oven
- refrigerator
- stove or hot plate

METRIC CONVERSION CHART

Use this handy chart to convert recipes to the metric system. If you can't find the conversion you need, ask an adult to help you find an online calculator!

STANDARD	METRIC
¼ teaspoon	1.2 milliliters
½ teaspoon	2.5 ml
¾ teaspoon	3.7 ml
1 teaspoon	5 ml
2 teaspoons	10 ml
1 tablespoon	15 ml
¼ cup	59 ml
⅓ cup	79 ml
½ cup	118 ml
⅔ cup	158 ml
¾ cup	177 ml
1 cup	237 ml

150 degrees Fahrenheit	66 degrees Celsius
300°F	149°C
350°F	177°C
400°F	204°C

1 ounce	28 grams
1 fluid ounce	30 milliliters
1 inch	2.5 centimeters
1 pound	0.5 kilograms

MAKING SWEETS SICKENING

Disgusting Descriptions

Gag-worthy names can turn an everyday **edible** into something really revolting. Once an ingredient or dish gets a disgusting name, it is hard to imagine it as anything else! Blobs of candy become bits of kitty poo. Gelatin turns to slimy snot globs.

Think about your ingredients as you create your desserts. Do any inspire you to give them stomach-churning names? Make labels for your sweets. Or tell your guests the title of each dessert as you serve it. Your diners' looks of horror are half the fun!

Sickening Setups

Nasty names make regular recipes revolting. But presentation is also important. And it's a lot of fun! Arrange your dishes to look like the disgusting things you call them. Then use fun props to set up a supergross scene. A box of bandages can make a blood-splattered cake even more believable. Fake bugs might make your worm dessert look even grosser. Whatever props you use, make sure they are **sanitized** first. And remove any props before serving food to guests. Keep your desserts fun and delicious without putting diners in danger.

MEAT TREATS

These tasty treats look like they came straight from the butcher's shop.

Serves: 4
Preparation Time: 10–30 minutes

Ingredients

3 tablespoons butter
1 10-ounce bag mini marshmallows
1 teaspoon vanilla extract
several drops red food coloring
6 cups crispy rice cereal
¾ cup strawberry or raspberry jam

Tools

- large stockpot
- measuring spoons
- measuring cups
- rubber spatula or mixing spoon
- 13 x 9-inch baking pan
- waxed paper
- knife

1. With an adult's help, melt the butter in the stockpot over low heat. Add the marshmallows, and cook until melted and smooth, stirring constantly.

2. Add the vanilla extract and food coloring. Stir together until the mixture is a light red color.

3

3. Remove the pot from heat. Stir in the cereal until all pieces are coated in the marshmallow mixture. Add the jam and stir some more.

4. Cover the bottom and sides of a baking pan with waxed paper. Pour the cereal mixture into the pan.

4

5. Cover the cereal with another sheet of waxed paper and press down firmly until the cereal is packed and even. Allow it to cool for 10 to 15 minutes.

6. Cut the cereal into squares, then gently shape each square into a patty, so it looks like a raw hamburger. Now watch your diners gobble up your sweet meat treats!

6

BIG OL' BOWL OF SNOT

**What's green and slimy and very sweet?
A bowl of mucus, of course!**

**Serves: 4
Preparation Time: 4 hours
(1 hour active)**

Ingredients

4 bananas
1 6-ounce package instant lime
  gelatin
½ cup small pineapple chunks
½ cup raisins

Tools

- mixing bowls
- fork
- measuring cups
- mixing spoon
- serving bowls

1. Put the bananas in a large bowl and mash them with a fork. Add 1 cup of hot water and stir together.

2. In another large bowl, make the lime gelatin according to the package instructions.

3. Add the banana mixture to the gelatin. Stir in the pineapple chunks and raisins.

4. Put the bowl in the refrigerator, and let it chill for at least 3 hours.

5. Spoon the mixture into individual bowls, and your snot is ready to slurp up!

POISONED ROTTEN APPLE

This tempting fruit looks good enough to eat—if you dare.

Serves: 4
Preparation Time: 1 hour (30 minutes active)

Ingredients

4 apples
1 12-ounce package of semi-sweet
   chocolate chips
¼ teaspoon salt
1 teaspoon black gel food coloring

Tools

• baking sheet
• parchment paper
• plate
• 4 clean wooden craft sticks
• small saucepan
• rubber spatula
• measuring spoons

1. Cover a baking sheet with parchment paper and set aside. Wash and dry the apples. Remove the apple stems. Place the apples upside down on a plate. Hold an apple with one hand, and push a craft stick into the center. Push it in about three-quarters of the way, rotating gently as you go. Repeat with the remaining apples.

2. Put the chocolate chips in the saucepan. With an adult's help, melt the chips over low heat, stirring constantly. Once the chips are melted, stir in the salt.

3. Remove the pan from the heat, and add several drops of food coloring. Stir the chocolate sauce until it is very dark, adding more food coloring if needed.

4. Hold an apple by the stick. Swirl it in the chocolate until the sides of the apple are coated in sauce.

5. Hold the apple above the pan to let any excess chocolate drip off. Then carefully set it on the prepared baking sheet.

6. Repeat steps 4 and 5 with the remaining apples. Then refrigerate them for 30 minutes. Watch your guests cringe as they take a bite out of these deadly-looking but delicious treats.

USED BANDAGE DELIGHTS

Gross out your family and friends with these bloody bandage treats.

Serves: 6–8
Preparation Time: 10 minutes

Ingredients

4 graham crackers
8 mini marshmallows
2 tablespoons raspberry jam

Tools

- knife
- cutting board
- microwave-safe plate
- measuring spoons
- table knife
- serving plate

1

1. Carefully cut or break apart the graham crackers along the seams.

2. Cut each marshmallow in half.

3. Place the graham crackers on a microwave-safe plate. Place a marshmallow slice in the middle of each cracker.

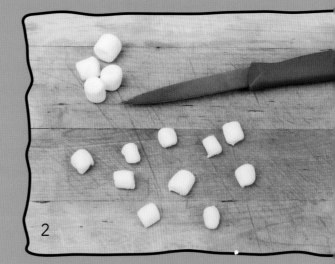

2

4. Spread a small amount of jam on top of each marshmallow.

5. Heat the graham crackers and marshmallows in the microwave for 30 seconds. The marshmallows should just begin to ooze.

6. Arrange your bandages on a serving plate, and let these gag-worthy snacks disgust your diners!

3

CAT LiTTER CAKE

This cat poo cake will have guests meowing for seconds.

Serves: 10
Preparation Time: 1½ hours
(30 minutes active)

Ingredients

Cakes

1 16.5-ounce chocolate cake mix
⅓ cup oil (or amount on cake mix package)
3 large eggs (or amount on cake mix package)
1 16.5-ounce yellow cake mix
⅓ cup oil (or amount on cake mix package)
3 large eggs (or amount on cake mix package)

Pudding

1 5.1-ounce package vanilla instant pudding mix
2 cups cold milk (or amount on pudding package)

15–20 white sandwich cookies
12 small Tootsie Rolls, unwrapped

Tools

- mixing bowls
- measuring cups
- measuring spoons
- mixing spoon
- 2 13 x 9-inch baking pans
- oven mitts
- **whisk**
- blender
- microwave-safe bowl
- serving dish or bowl

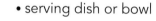

1. **Preheat** the oven to the temperature on the cake mix packages. Make both cakes according to the package directions. When they are done baking, let the cakes cool.

2. Whisk together the pudding mix and milk in a bowl. Then chill the pudding in the refrigerator for 10 minutes or until the pudding is thick.

1

3. Put two handfuls of cookies in a blender, and blend on the low setting until the cookies are crumbled.

4. Crumble the cakes into a large bowl. Add in half of the crumbled cookies. Mix in the pudding a few tablespoons at a time until all the crumbs are combined. You may not need all the pudding.

3

5. Put the Tootsie Rolls in a microwave-safe bowl. Microwave them on high for 15 seconds at a time. Stop when the rolls are easy to bend, but not completely melted. Then shape the Tootsie Rolls into poo-shaped pieces. Be careful! The Tootsie Rolls may be hot.

6. Transfer the cake mixture to a serving dish or bowl. Arrange the Tootsie Rolls in and on top of the cake. The sight of this crumbly cake may make some guests gag, but the taste will leave them wanting more!

4

TIP

To check if a cake is done, slide a toothpick or clean table knife into it. If the knife or toothpick comes out clean, your cake is fully cooked.

SWEET WORMS IN DIRT

Creepy-crawly worms buried in cookie dirt make a perfect wriggly snack.

Serves: 6–8
Preparation Time: 5½ hours
(30 minutes active)

Ingredients

2 6-ounce packages instant
   raspberry gelatin
3 packets unflavored gelatin
   powder
1 cup whipping cream
15 drops green food coloring
30–40 chocolate sandwich cookies

Tools

- measuring cups
- saucepan
- large mixing bowl
- mixing spoons or spatulas
- 1 large package bendable straws
- tall, narrow container with a flat
     bottom, such as a vase
- cup with a spout
- rolling pin
- baking sheet
- large plastic bag
- serving bowl or plate

1. With an adult's help, **boil** 2¾ cups water in a saucepan over medium-high heat. Pour the hot water into a mixing bowl. Then stir in the raspberry and unflavored gelatin.

2. Let the mixture cool for 20 minutes or until it is **lukewarm**. Then mix in the whipping cream and green food coloring.

2

3. Arrange the straws in the container so the straws' ends are **flush** with the bottom. Pack the container very tightly so it is completely full. Carefully pour the gelatin mixture into the straws, filling them all the way to the top. Refrigerate the container for 4 hours, until the gelatin is firm.

4. Using a rolling pin, roll over the straws to loosen the gelatin worms. Then use your fingers to carefully squeeze the worms out onto a baking sheet. Refrigerate for another hour.

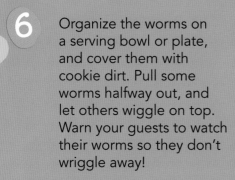

3

5. Seal the cookies in a large plastic bag. Crush the cookies by rolling them with a rolling pin. The cookies will be your dirt!

6. Organize the worms on a serving bowl or plate, and cover them with cookie dirt. Pull some worms halfway out, and let others wiggle on top. Warn your guests to watch their worms so they don't wriggle away!

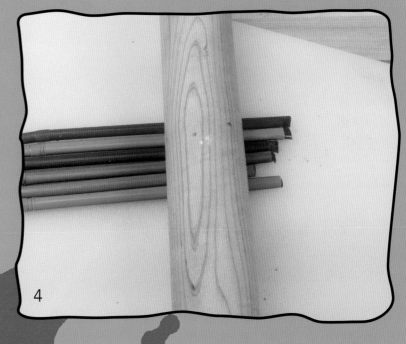

4

BLOOD SUCKERS

This gruesome dessert is the perfect on-the-go treat for vampire-loving friends and family.

Serves: 10–12
Preparation Time:
30–45 minutes

Ingredients

10–15 maraschino cherries
red food coloring
2 cups granulated sugar
4 tablespoons light corn syrup

Tools

- knife
- cutting board
- small bowl
- baking sheet
- parchment paper
- 15 white lollipop sticks
- measuring cups
- measuring spoons
- small saucepan
- candy thermometer
- large bowl

1. Chop the cherries and put them in a small bowl. Then mix in several drops of food coloring.

2. Cover a baking sheet with parchment paper. Space the lollipop sticks on the baking sheet about 3 inches apart. The sticks should all face the same direction.

3. With an adult's help, bring the sugar, corn syrup, and ¼ cup of water to a boil in a saucepan over medium heat. This makes a liquid candy mixture. Let the mixture boil for 5 to 7 minutes, and test the temperature with a candy thermometer. The mixture is done when it is 300° to 310°F.

4. Fill a large bowl with ice water. With an adult's help, place the saucepan in the bowl. Let the pan sit in the ice water for 20 to 30 seconds. Then stir the mixture for 1 minute.

5. Have an adult help with this step. The liquid candy is very hot! Scoop 1 tablespoon of the liquid candy on top of each lollipop stick. Once you have candy puddles around each stick, place a drop or two of cherry mixture in the center of each puddle. Then add several drops of food coloring to each puddle. The candy hardens quickly, so you will need to work fast.

6. Let the candy cool for 10 minutes. Then watch your guests' looks of disgust as they lick up these bloody suckers.

If you don't have a candy thermometer, scoop out ½ teaspoon of liquid candy and drop it into cold water. Then take it out right away. If it's done, the candy should separate into threads.

ALIEN LIMB

Create an alien autopsy scene that tastes amazing!

Serves: 6
Preparation Time: 2–3 hours
(30 minutes active)

Ingredients

2 6-ounce packages instant gelatin,
    any flavor
1 cup canned pears
1 cup pineapple chunks
red licorice
1 cup grapes

Tools

• newspaper
• masking tape
• aluminum foil
• baking pan
• plastic wrap
• measuring cups
• mixing bowls
• mixing spoons
• serving dish
• knife
• cutting board

1. Roll several newspaper sheets into a cone shape. Use masking tape to attach more newspaper sheets to the cone. It should begin to look like a **tentacle**. Keep adding newspapers until the limb is the size you want. Wrap three to four pieces of foil around one half of the newspaper pages. This makes a mold.

1

2. Remove the newspaper and set the mold in the baking pan. Curve the foil if needed to fit the mold in the pan. Cover the inside of the mold with plastic wrap.

3. Mix together both batches of gelatin in separate bowls according to the packages' instructions. Pour one batch into your mold. Keep the second batch in the mixing bowl. Refrigerate both batches for 30 to 40 minutes or until firm.

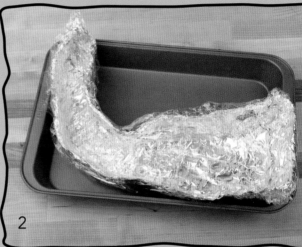

2

4. Remove the mold from the refrigerator, and decorate the gelatin limb with pieces of fruit and candy. Use pear pieces and pineapple chunks for bones. Licorice could be blood vessels. Get creative!

5. Melt the second batch of gelatin in the microwave for 30 seconds at a time until it is runny. Then pour it on top of the fruit. Refrigerate the gelatin for 1 to 2 hours.

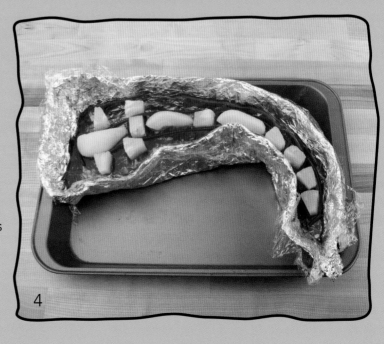

4

6. Remove the mold from the refrigerator. Place it upside-down in a serving dish. Carefully remove the mold from the gelatin. Then cut the grapes in half, and place them on the tentacle to look like suction cups. Your creepy alien arm is ready to serve!

BLOOD-SPLATTERED CAKE

This mess of a cake makes a terrifying treat for gore-loving guests.

Serves: 4–6
Preparation Time: 1½–2 hours (45 minutes active)

Ingredients

Cake

cooking spray
2 cups white sugar
1¾ cups all-purpose flour
¾ cup unsweetened cocoa powder
1½ teaspoons baking powder
1½ teaspoons baking soda
1 teaspoon salt
2 eggs
1 cup milk
½ cup vegetable oil
1 tablespoon vanilla extract
½ cup strawberry jam

Frosting

1 cup (2 sticks) unsalted butter, softened to room temperature
4 cups powdered sugar
4 tablespoons heavy whipping cream
2 tablespoons vanilla extract
¼ teaspoon salt

Blood-Splatter Sauce

3 tablespoons cornstarch
1 teaspoon red food coloring
1–2 drops green food coloring
1 teaspoon maple syrup

Tools

- 9-inch round cake pan
- 6-inch round cake pan
- measuring cups
- measuring spoons
- mixing bowls, various sizes
- mixing spoons
- saucepan
- mixer or hand mixer
- oven mitts
- toothpick or table knife
- wire cooling rack
- serving plate
- rubber spatula or table knife
- whisk
- newspaper
- brand-new toothbrush

1 Preheat the oven to 350°F. Coat the cake pans with cooking spray.

2 Start by making the cake. Stir together the sugar, flour, cocoa powder, baking powder, baking soda, and salt in a large mixing bowl. With an adult's help, bring 1 cup of water to a boil over medium-high heat.

2

3 Form a hole in the center of the dry cake ingredients, and add the eggs, milk, oil, and vanilla to the hole. Using the mixer on medium speed, blend together all the ingredients for 3 minutes. With an adult's help, add the boiling water. Then mix until all the ingredients are combined.

3

4 Pour the **batter** into the cake pans and bake for 20 to 30 minutes or until done. Insert a toothpick or table knife into the cakes to check if they are done. If the toothpick or knife comes out clean, the cake is fully cooked. Remove the cake from the oven to cool for 10 to 15 minutes. Then flip the cakes out onto a wire rack, and cool for 1 hour.

5 While the cakes are cooling, make the frosting. Put the butter in a mixing bowl and mix it on low speed for 3 to 5 minutes. Remember to clean the mixer parts between uses. Stop when the butter is creamy and pale.

6 Add the powdered sugar, ½ cup at a time. Then mix in the heavy cream, one teaspoon at a time. If the frosting is too runny, add more powdered sugar. If it is too stiff, add more cream.

6

Blood-Splattered Cake continued next page

TIP

If you don't have a 6-inch cake pan, use two 9-inch cake pans. Then use a knife and circular object, such as a bowl, as a template to cut one cake to the size you want.

Blood-Splattered Cake, continued

7 Add the vanilla and salt to the frosting mixture. Beat with the mixer on medium-high speed for 3 to 4 minutes.

8 Place the larger cake on a serving plate. Spread the jam in a circle in the center of the cake. Then set the smaller cake on top of the jam.

9 Use a rubber spatula or table knife to gently spread the frosting all over the cake. Be careful not to let the spatula pick up any crumbs. Then let the frosting dry for 20 to 30 minutes.

10 Next whisk all blood-splatter sauce ingredients together in a small bowl with 1 tablespoon of water.

11 The next step is messy, so cover your work surface with newspaper. You may even want to set up the newspaper outside if the weather is nice. Set the serving plate and cake on top of the newspaper.

12 Coat the toothbrush bristles in the sauce. Then flick the toothbrush at the cake. This should splatter the sauce all over the cake. Repeat until your cake has enough splatter. Dribble the rest of the sauce down the sides of the cake. Tell your guests to watch out for severed fingers as they dig into this disgusting dessert!

WRAPPING UP

Cleaning Up

Once you are done cooking, it is time to clean up! Make sure to wipe up spills, wash dishes, and clear the table. Wash and put away any props you used that don't belong in the kitchen. Make sure any leftovers are properly packaged and refrigerated.

Keep Cooking!

Get inspired by the disgusting desserts you made. Think of ways to create your own versions of these sickening yet sweet treats. Or dream up your own horrifying dessert recipes! Think gross, and keep on cooking!

GLOSSARY

batter: a thin mixture containing flour, eggs, oil, or other ingredients that is used to make baked goods

boil: to heat a liquid until it gives off steam and bubbles

edible: something that can be safely eaten

flush: even or level with something

lukewarm: a little bit warm

preheat: to heat an oven to the required temperature before putting in the food

sanitized: cleaned so something is free of germs

template: a shape that can be used as guide to making the same shape

tentacle: a long, flexible limb on some animals, such as jellyfish, octopus, or squid

whisk: to stir very quickly using a fork or a tool made of curved wire, also called a whisk

FURTHER INFORMATION

Cornell, Kari. *Dandy Desserts.*
Minneapolis: Millbrook Press, 2014.
These easy-to-follow recipes will have beginning bakers making sweet treats in no time!

Halloween Recipes for Kids
http://www.kraftrecipes.com/recipes/holidays-and-entertaining/holidays/halloween/kids-party-menu.aspx
The Halloween-themed treats on this site are perfect for a spooky celebration any time of the year.

Kuskowski, Alex. *Super Simple Holiday Cookies: Easy Cookie Recipes for Kids!*
Minneapolis: Abdo Publishing, 2016.
Try out these easy cookies recipes for some tasty holiday treats.

Recipes: Dessert
http://www.superhealthykids.com/recipe-category/dessert/
Check out these fun and healthful desserts perfect for new chefs.

INDEX